100 years of Popular Music

RDS

1900 1920 1930 1940 1950 1960 1970 1980 **1990** 2000

90s

Product Line Manager:
Carol Cuellar

Project Manager:
Zobeida Pérez

Book Cover and Design:
JPCreativeGroup.com

CONTENTS

Title	Artist	Page
All for Love	Bryan Adams, Sting & Rod Stewart	4
All I Wanna Do	Sheryl Crow	10
Amazed	Lonestar	18
Angel of Mine	Monica	22
...Baby One More Time	Britney Spears	28
Back at One	Brian McKnight	33
Because of You	98°	38
Because You Loved Me	Celine Dion	43
Believe	Cher	48
Breathe	Faith Hill	53
Can't Stop This Thing We Started	Bryan Adams	58
Don't Speak	No Doubt	63
Dreaming of You	Selena	68
End of the Road	Boyz II Men	74
Fantasy	Mariah Carey	82
Finally	Ce Ce Peniston	252
From This Moment On	Shania Twain	88
Genie in a Bottle	Christina Aguilera	95
Have I Told You Lately	Rod Stewart	100
Hold On	Wilson Phillips	105
How Do I Live	LeAnn Rimes	110
I Believe I Can Fly	R. Kelly	118
I Cross My Heart	George Strait	114
(Everything I Do) I Do It for You	Bryan Adams	123

CONTENTS

Title	Artist	Page

Title	Artist	Page
I Don't Have the Heart	James Ingram	128
I Will Always Love You	Whitney Houston	131
I'll Be There for You (Theme From "Friends")	The Rembrandts	136
I'll Remember	Madonna	142
Insensitive	Jann Arden	146
Ironic	Alanis Morissette	152
Just Another Day	Jon Secada	158
Live for Loving You	Gloria Estefan	163
Livin' La Vida Loca	Ricky Martin	168
Macarena	Los Del Rio	180
Man! I Feel Like a Woman!	Shania Twain	186
Music of My Heart	Gloria Estefan & ★NSYNC	192
Quit Playing Games (With My Heart)	Backstreet Boys	175
Run-Around	Blues Traveler	198
Save the Best for Last	Vanessa Williams	206
Smooth	Santana featuring Rob Thomas	211
Stay (I Missed You)	Lisa Loeb	216
This Kiss	Faith Hill	222
2 Become 1	Spice Girls	226
Un-Break My Heart	Toni Braxton	231
Valentine	Jim Brickman with Martina McBride	236
Waiting for Tonight	Jennifer Lopez	242
Where Does My Heart Beat Now	Celine Dion	247
You Were Meant for Me	Jewel	77

4

From the Original Motion Picture Soundtrack "THE THREE MUSKETEERS"

ALL FOR LOVE

Written by
BRYAN ADAMS, ROBERT JOHN "MUTT" LANGE
and MICHAEL KAMEN

8

(Instrumental solo . . .

. . . end solo)

Now, it's

Chorus:

all for___ one, all for love.___ Let the one you hold be the one you___

want, the one you___ need. 'Cause when it's all for___ one, it's one for all.

ALL I WANNA DO

Words and Music by SHERYL CROW, WYN COOPER,
BILL BOTTRELL, DAVID BAERWALD and KEVIN GILBERT

All I Wanna Do - 8 - 1

14

Verse 3:
I like a good beer buzz early in the morning,
And Billy likes to peel the labels from his bottles of Bud
And shred them on the bar.
Then he lights every match in an oversized pack,
Letting each one burn down to his thick fingers
Before blowing and cursing them out.
And he's watching the Buds as they spin on the floor.
A happy couple enters the bar dancing dangerously close to one another.
The bartender looks up from his want ads.
(To Chorus:)

AMAZED

Verse 2:
The smell of your skin,
The taste of your kiss,
The way you whisper in the dark.
Your hair all around me,
Baby, you surround me;
You touch every place in my heart.
Oh, it feels like the first time every time.
I wanna spend the whole night in your eyes.
(To Chorus:)

ANGEL OF MINE

Words and Music by
RHETT LAWRENCE and TRAVON POTTS

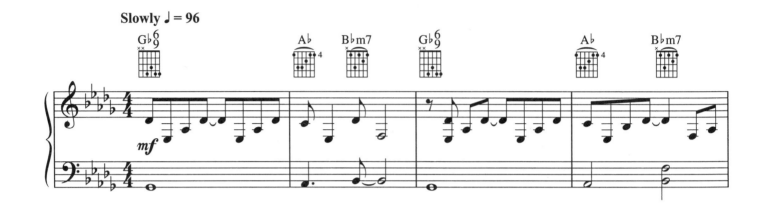

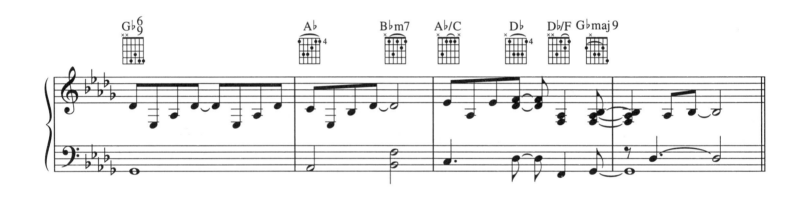

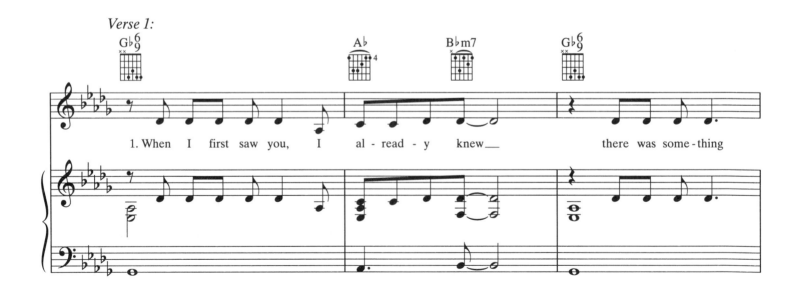

Verse 1:

1. When I first saw you, I al-read-y knew___ there was some-thing

Angel of Mine - 6 - 2

...BABY ONE MORE TIME

Words and Music by
MAX MARTIN

To Coda ⊕

Hit me, ba-by, one more time. I must con-fess_____ that my lone-li-ness_____ is kill-ing me now._____

_____ Don't you know I still___ be-lieve___ that you will be here___

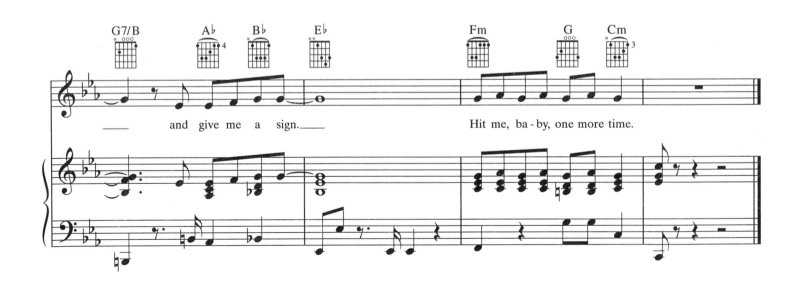

____ and give me a sign.____ Hit me, ba-by, one more time.

BACK AT ONE

Words and Music by
BRIAN McKNIGHT

BECAUSE OF YOU

Words and Music by
ANDERS BAGGE, ARNTHOR BIRGISSON,
CHRISTIAN KARLSSON and PATRICK TUCKER

Repeat ad lib. and fade

Verse 2:
Honestly, could it be you and me
Like it was before, need less or more?
'Cause when I close my eyes
At night, I realize that no one else
Could ever take your place.
I still can feel, and it's so real,
When you're touching me,
Kisses endlessly.
It's just a place in the sun
Where our love's begun.
I miss you, yes, I miss you.
(To Chorus:)

BECAUSE YOU LOVED ME
(Theme from "Up Close & Personal")

Words and Music by
DIANE WARREN

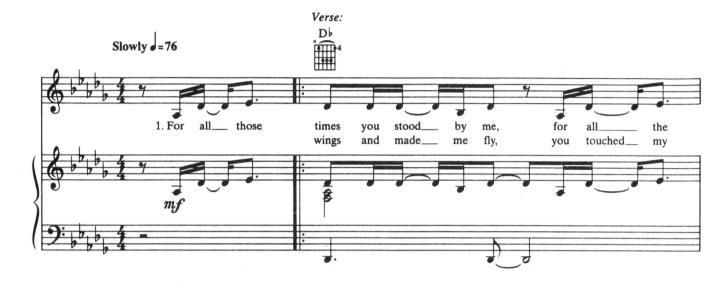

Because You Loved Me - 5 - 1

BELIEVE

Words and Music by
BRIAN HIGGINS, STUART McLENNAN,
PAUL BARRY, STEPHEN TORCH,
MATT GRAY and TIM POWELL

* Original recording in G♭ major.

52

BREATHE

Words and Music by
STEPHANIE BENTLEY
and HOLLY LAMAR

Slowly ♩ = 60

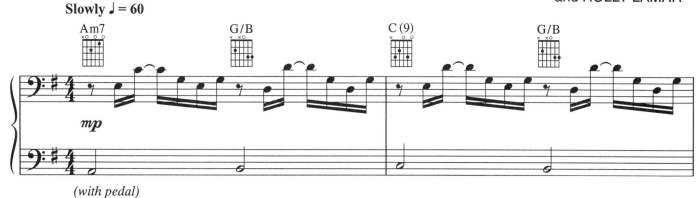

(with pedal)

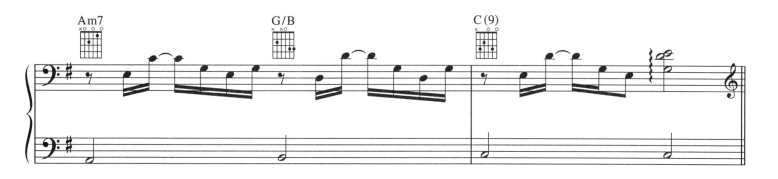

Verse 1:

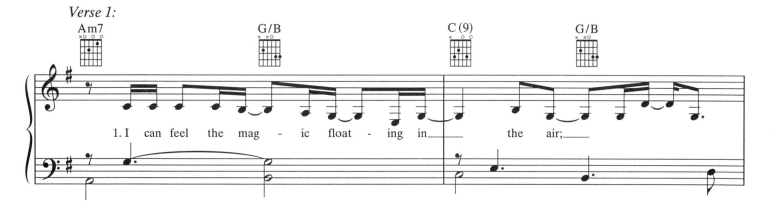

1. I can feel the mag - ic float - ing in___ the air;___

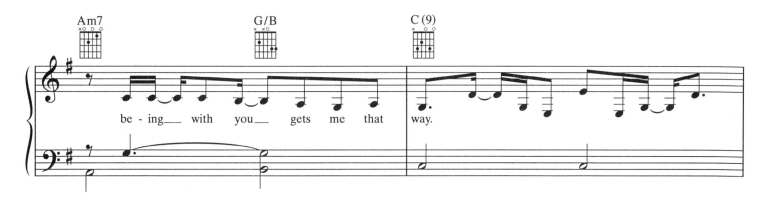

be - ing___ with you___ gets me that way.

Breathe - 5 - 1

54

Chorus:

56

1.
C (9)
G/B
Am7
D7sus
G
Am7
breathe.
cresc.
mf
Just
breathe.
C (9)
Dsus
D
G
Am7
C (9)
Dsus
2.
C (9)
G/B
Am7
D7sus
breathe.
cresc.
mf
Just
G
Am7
C (9)
Dsus
D
G
Am7
breathe.
C (9)
D7sus
G
Am7
Caught up in the touch, the slow and stead-y rush. And, ba-by, is-n't

CAN'T STOP THIS THING WE STARTED

Lyrics and Music by
BRYAN ADAMS and R.J. LANGE

Oh,   why take   it   slow?_____

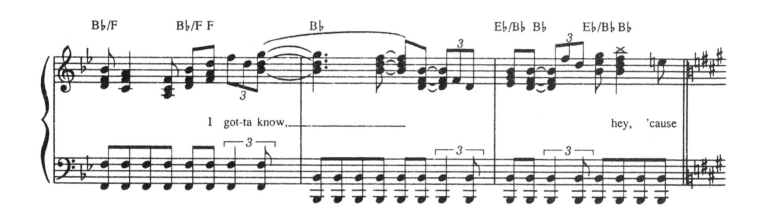

I got-ta know,_____   hey, 'cause

noth - ing can   stop   this   thing that we've got.   (Instrumental solo . . .

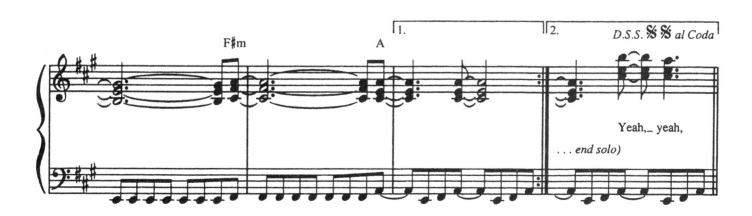

Yeah,_ yeah,

. . . end solo)

62

DON'T SPEAK

Moderately

Words and Music by
ERIC STEFANI and GWEN STEFANI

66

Don't Speak - 5 - 4

DREAMING OF YOU

Words and Music by
TOM SNOW and
FRANNE GOLDE

Moderately ♩ = 88

mp

(with pedal)

Verse:

1. Late at night when all the world___ is sleep-ing, I stay up and think of you.___ And I

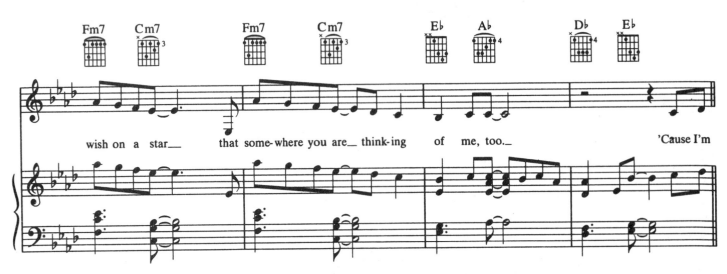

wish on a star___ that some-where you are___ think-ing of me, too.___ 'Cause I'm

Dreaming of You - 6 - 1

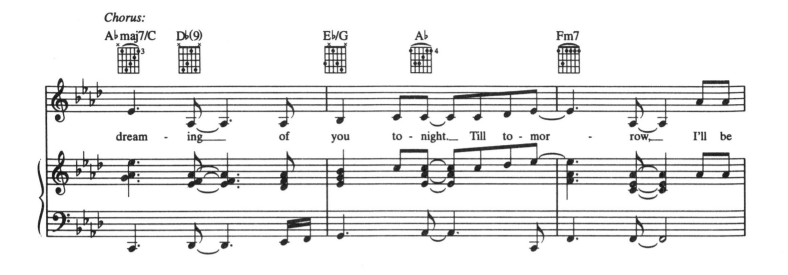

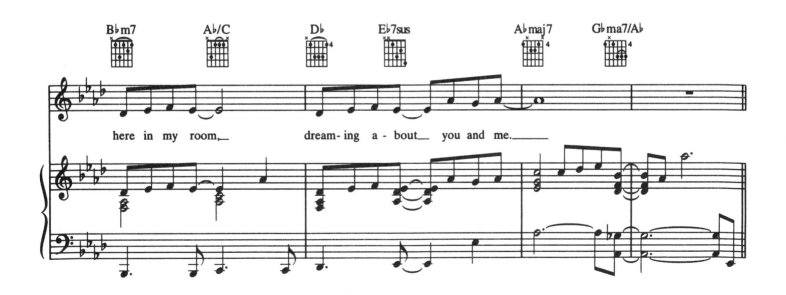

70

Dreaming of You - 6 - 3

72

Dreaming of You - 6 - 5

END OF THE ROAD

Words and Music by
BABYFACE, L.A. REID, DARYL SIMMONS

End of the Road - 3 - 2

Come to the end of the_ road,_ still I can't let_ you

go._ It's un-nat-ur-al. You be-long to me, I be-long to you._

-long to me, I be-long to you. Al-though we've | -long to me, I be-long to you._

Verse 2:
Girl, I know you really love me, you just don't realize.
You've never been there before, it's only your first time.
Maybe I'll forgive you, mmm. . . maybe you'll try.
We should be happy together, forever, you and I.

Bridge 2:
Could you love me again like you loved me before?
This time, I want you to love me much more.
This time, instead just come back to my bed.
And baby, just don't let me down.

Verse 3, spoken:
Girl I'm here for you.
All those times at night when you just hurt me,
And just ran out with that other fellow,
Baby, I knew about it.
I just didn't care.
You just don't understand how much I love you, do you?
I'm here for you.
I'm not out to go out there and cheat all night just like you did, baby.
But that's alright, huh, I love you anyway.
And I'm still gonna be here for you 'til my dyin' day, baby.
Right now, I'm just in so much pain, baby,
'Cause you just won't come back to me, will you?
Just come back to me.

Bridge 3, spoken:
Yes, baby, my heart is lonely.
My heart hurts, baby, yes, I feel pain too.
Baby please . . .

YOU WERE MEANT FOR ME

Words and Music by
JEWEL KILCHER and STEVE POLTZ

You Were Meant for Me - 5 - 1

78

81

Verse 2:

I called my mama, she was out for a walk.
Consoled a cup of coffee, but it didn't wanna talk.
So I picked up a paper, it was more bad news,
More hearts being broken or people being used.
Put on my coat in the pouring rain.
I saw a movie, it just wasn't the same,
'Cause it was happy and I was sad,
And it made me miss you, oh, so bad.
(To Chorus:)

Verse 3:

I brush my teeth and put the cap back on,
I know you hate it when I leave the light on.
I pick a book up and then I turn the sheets down,
And then I take a breath and a good look around.
Put on my pj's and hop into bed.
I'm half alive but I feel mostly dead.
I try and tell myself it'll be all right,
I just shouldn't think anymore tonight.
(To Chorus:)

You Were Meant for Me - 5 - 5

FANTASY

Words and Music by
DAVE HALL, MARIAH CAREY, CHRIS FRANTZ,
TINA WEYMOUTH, ADRIAN BELEW
and STEVEN STANLEY

Fantasy - 6 - 1

Verse 2:
Images of rapture
Creep into me slowly,
As you're going to my head.
And my heart beats faster
When you take me over,
Time and time and time again.
But it's just a...
(To Chorus:)

FROM THIS MOMENT ON

Words and Music by
SHANIA TWAIN and R.J. LANGE

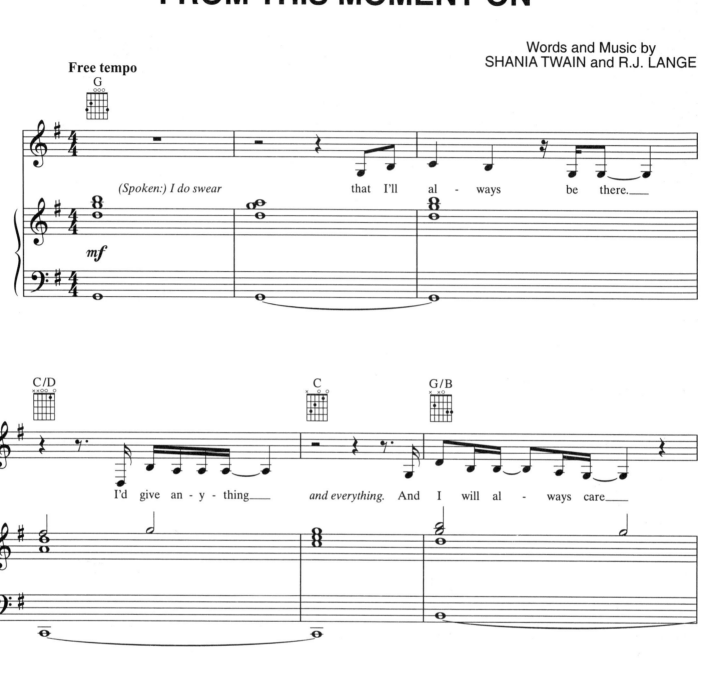

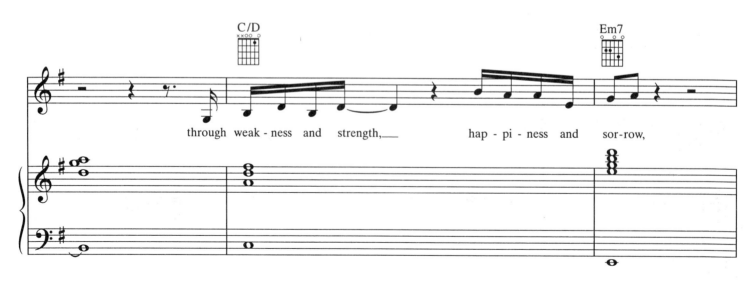

From This Moment On - 7 - 1

Slowly ♩ = 72
Verse 1:

ing   I would-n't give,_____   from this   mo-ment on.___

You're the rea-son I___ be-lieve_ in

love._____   And you're the an-swer to___ my prayers_ from

94

GENIE IN A BOTTLE

Words and Music by
PAMELA SHEYNE, DAVID FRANK
and STEVE KIPNER

Chorus:

HAVE I TOLD YOU LATELY

Words and Music by
VAN MORRISON

Slowly, with expression

Have I told ___ you late-ly that I love you? *Have I*

told you there's no one else ___ a-bove ___ you?

Fill my heart ___ with glad-ness, *take a-way all ___ my sad-ness,*

Have I Told You Lately - 5 - 1

to the one. ___ And have I told _____ you late - ly that I love you? Have I told you there's no one else ___ a - bove you? You fill my heart ___ with glad - ness, take a - way ___ my sad - ness, ease my trou - bles that's ___ what you

104

Have I Told You Lately - 5 - 5

HOLD ON

Words and Music by
GLEN BALLARD, CARNIE WILSON
and CHYNNA PHILLIPS

Hold On - 5 - 1

From the Touchstone Motion Picture "CON AIR"

HOW DO I LIVE

Words and Music by
DIANE WARREN

How Do I Live - 4 - 1

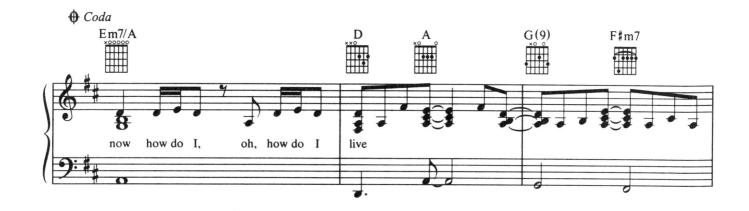

now how do I,   oh, how do I   live

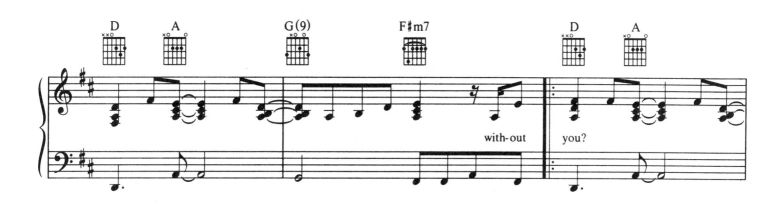

with-out   you?

Repeat ad lib. and fade
(vocal 1st time only)

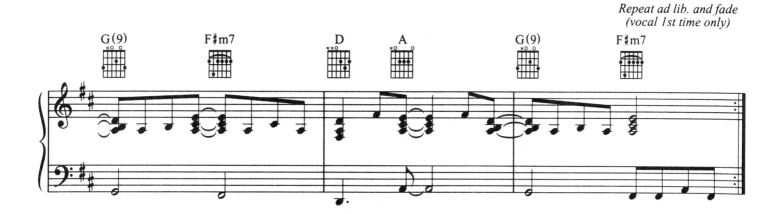

Verse 2:
Without you, there'd be no sun in my sky,
There would be no love in my life,
There'd be no world left for me.
And I, baby, I don't know what I would do,
I'd be lost if I lost you.
If you ever leave,
Baby, you would take away everything real in my life.
And tell me now...
(To Chorus:)

I CROSS MY HEART

Words and Music by
STEVE DORFF and ERIC KAZ

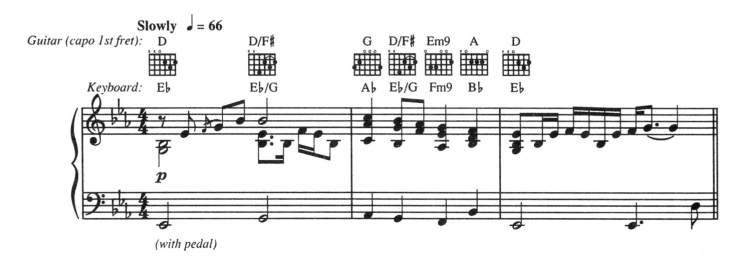

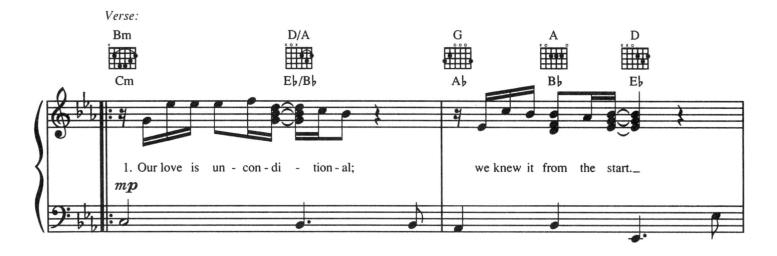

1. Our love is un-con-di - tion-al; we knew it from the start.

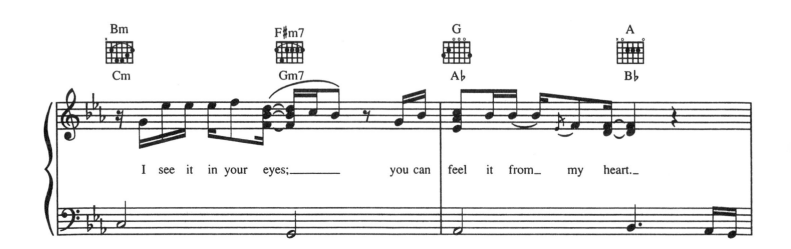

I see it in your eyes;_____ you can feel it from__ my heart.__

I Cross My Heart - 4 - 1

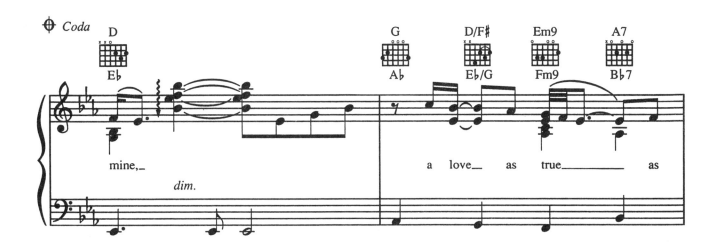

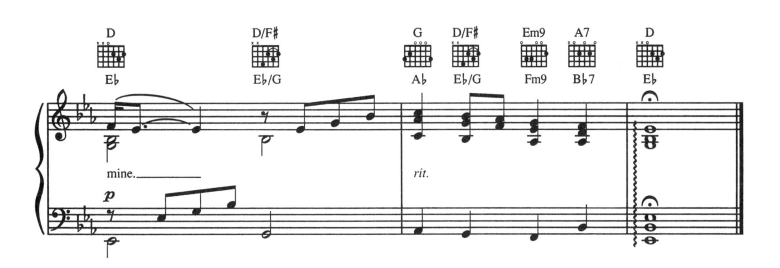

Verse 2:
You will always be the miracle
That makes my life complete;
And as long as there's a breath in me,
I'll make yours just as sweet.
As we look into the future,
It's as far as we can see,
So let's make each tomorrow
Be the best that it can be.
(To Chorus:)

I BELIEVE I CAN FLY

Words and Music by
R. KELLY

Verse:

used to think_ that I_ could not_ go on, and life was noth-ing but_ an aw-ful

I was on_ the verge_ of break-ing down. Some-times si - lence can seem_ so

I Believe I Can Fly - 5 - 1

120

I Believe I Can Fly - 5 - 3

From the Motion Picture "Robin Hood: Prince Of Thieves"

(EVERYTHING I DO) I DO IT FOR YOU

Lyrics and Music by
BRYAN ADAMS, ROBERT JOHN LANGE
and MICHAEL KAMEN

(Everything I Do) I Do It for You - 5 - 1

124

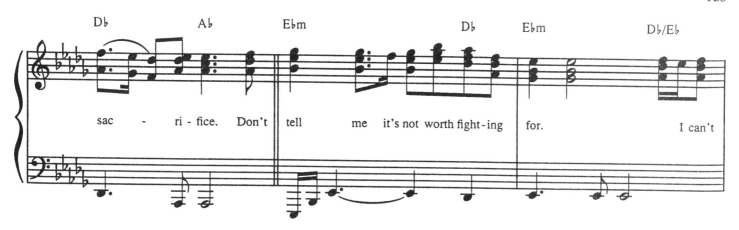

sac - ri - fice. Don't tell me it's not worth fight-ing for. I can't

help it, there's noth-ing I want more. You know it's true,_____ ev-ery-thing I__

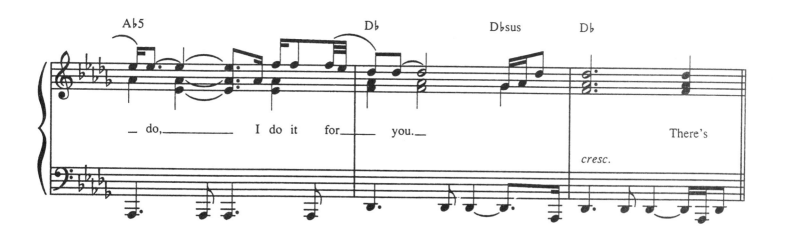

__ do,_____ I do it for____ you.____ There's

no love_____ like your love,_____ and no__ oth - er could give

(Everything I Do) I Do It for You - 5 - 3

more___ love. There's no - where___ un - less you're_ there, all the

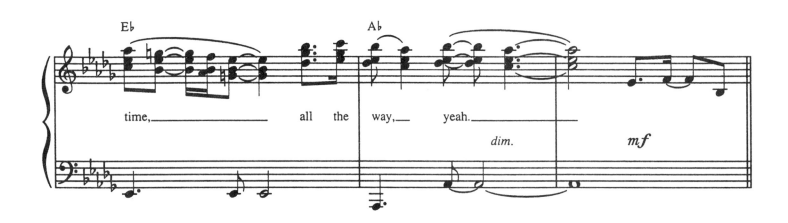

time,_____ all the way,___ yeah._____

dim.   *mf*

(instrumental solo . . .

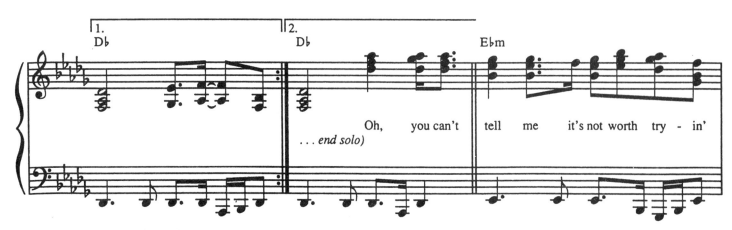

1.   2.

Oh, you can't tell me it's not worth try - in'
. . . end solo)

for.___ I can't help___ it, there's noth-ing I want more. Yeah,__ I would

cresc. *f*

fight_ for you,__ I'd lie__ for you,__ walk the wire__ for you,__ yeah,__ I'd

die for__ you._____ You know it's true, ev-ery-thing I__

dim. *mp*

_ do,____ oh,____ I do it for___ you.____

rit. *dim.* *p*

I DON'T HAVE THE HEART

Words and Music by
JUD FRIEDMAN and ALLAN RICH

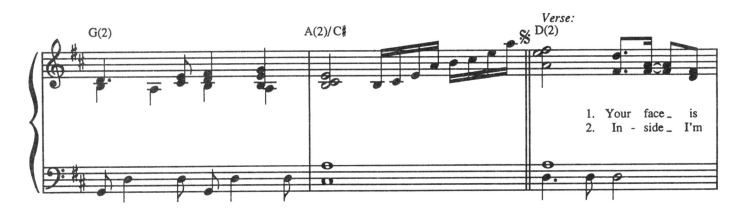

I Don't Have The Heart - 3 - 1

I Don't Have The Heart - 3 - 2

I WILL ALWAYS LOVE YOU

Words and Music by
DOLLY PARTON

132

134

I Will Always Love You - 5 - 4

Verse 3: Instrumental solo

Verse 4:
I hope life treats you kind
And I hope you have all you've dreamed of.
And I wish to you, joy and happiness.
But above all this, I wish you love.
(To Chorus:)

I'LL BE THERE FOR YOU
(Theme from "FRIENDS")

Words by
DAVID CRANE, MARTA KAUFFMAN, ALLEE WILLIS,
PHIL SOLEM and DANNY WILDE

Music by
MICHAEL SKLOFF

I'll Be There for You - 6 - 1

138

* Guitar fill reads 8va.

I'll Be There for You - 6 - 3

er know — me, no one could ev - er see — me.

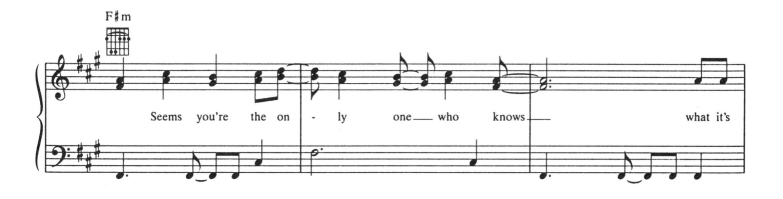

Seems you're the on - ly one — who knows — what it's

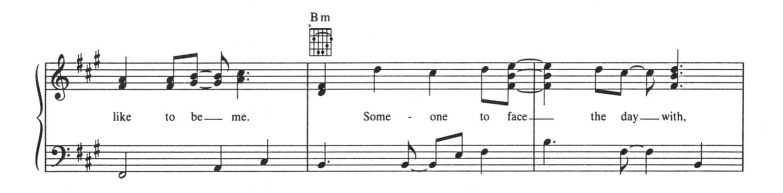

like to be — me. Some - one to face — the day — with,

make it through all — the rest — with, some - one I'll al -

I'll Be There for You - 6 - 6

142

Theme from the Motion Picture "WITH HONORS"

I'LL REMEMBER

Words and Music by
MADONNA CICCONE, PATRICK LEONARD
and RICHARD PAGE

144

INSENSITIVE

Words and Music by
ANNE LOREE

How do you cool ___ your lips
How do you numb ___ your skin

Insensitive - 6 - 1

148

Insensitive - 6 - 3

IRONIC

Lyrics by
ALANIS MORISSETTE

Music by
ALANIS MORISSETTE
and GLEN BALLARD

Ironic - 6 - 1

154

Ironic - 6 - 3

And life has a fun - ny way___ of help-ing you out___ when you think_ ev-'ry-thing's_ gone wrong_ and ev-'ry-thing blows_ up in_ your face.___

D.S. al Coda

A

CODA

meet-ing his beau - ti - ful wife.

And is - n't it i - ron - ic... don't you

mp

JUST ANOTHER DAY

Words and Music by
JON SECADA and MIGUEL A. MOREJON

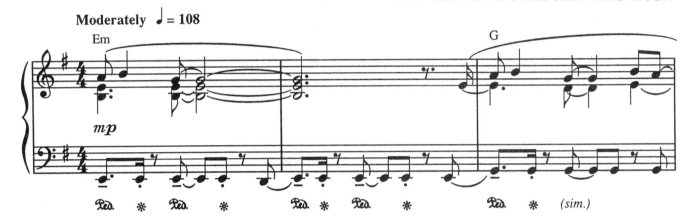

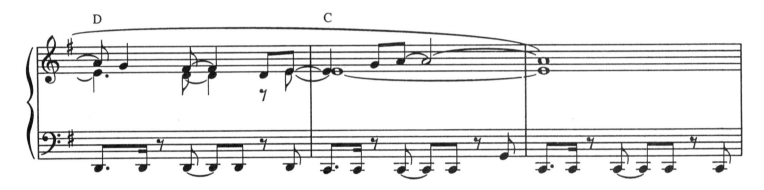

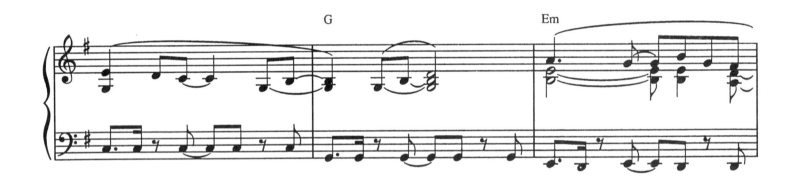

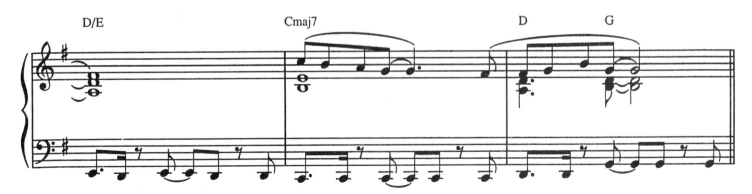

Just Another Day - 5 - 1

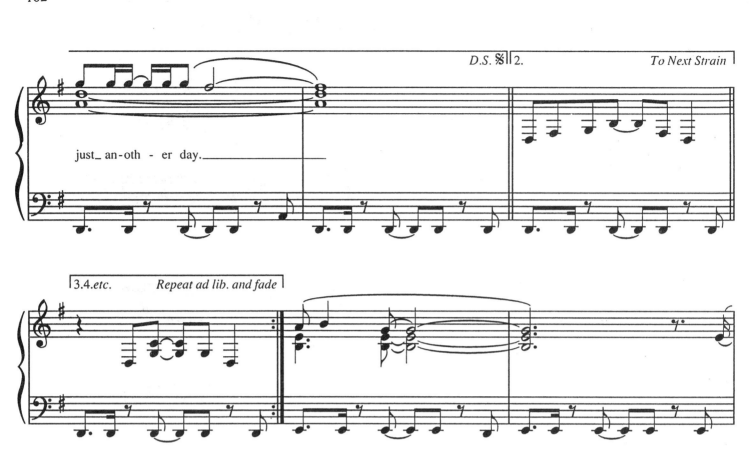

D.S. 𝄋 ‖ 2.   **To Next Strain**

just_ an-oth - er day._____

⌐3.4.*etc.*   *Repeat ad lib. and fade* ⌐

G   D   C

G   *D.S.S.* 𝄋 𝄋

Verse 2:
Making the time,
Find the right lines to make you stay forever.
What do I have to tell you?
Just trying to hold on to something.
    (Trying to hold on to something good.)
Give us a chance to make it.
    (Give us a chance to make it.)

Bridge 2:
Don't wanna hold on to never . . .
I'm not that strong, I'm not that strong.
(To Chorus:)

Bridge 3:
Why can't you stay forever?
Just give me a reason, give me a reason.
(To Chorus:)

LIVE FOR LOVING YOU

Words and Music by
GLORIA ESTEFAN, DIANE WARREN
and EMILIO ESTEFAN, JR.

Live For Loving You - 5 - 1

164

Live For Loving You - 5 - 3

166

Live For Loving You - 5 - 4

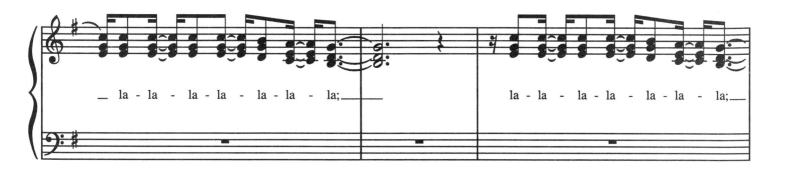

la - la - la - la - la - la - la - la;

la - la - la - la - la - la - la - la;

Baby, I   live   for   lov - ing

you._____   Ooh.,_____   la - la - la - la - la - la - la - la;

Repeat ad lib. and fade

Verse 2:
I find it hard to find the words
To say what I am feeling.
I'm so in love, I'm so alive,
And I know you're the reason why,
Why I'm so happy all the time.
Oh, I, I wonder, wonder, wonder why.
(To Bridge:)

Verse 3:
It would never cross my mind,
To find another lover.
'Cause after having been with you,
There could be no other.
I, just touching you I'm satisfied.
Oh, I, I wonder, wonder, wonder why.
(To Bridge:)

LIVIN' LA VIDA LOCA

Words and Music by
ROBI ROSA and DESMOND CHILD

Verse 1:

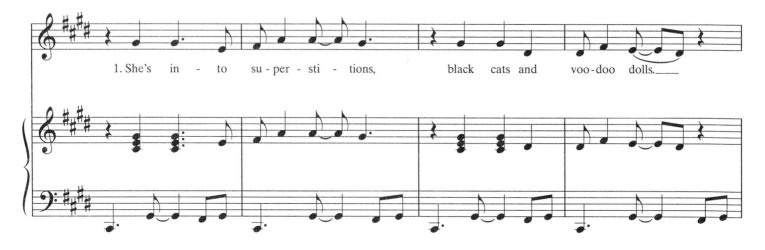

1. She's in-to su-per-sti-tions, black cats and voo-doo dolls.

Livin' la Vida Loca - 7 - 1

I feel a pre-mo-ni-tion, that girl's gon-na make me fall.____

Verses 2 & 3:

2. She's in - to new sen - sa - tions, new kicks in the can -dle - light.____
3. *See additional lyrics*

She's got a new ad - dic - tion for ev - 'ry day and night.____ 1. She'll

171

Livin' la Vida Loca - 7 - 4

172

Coda

2. Instrumental (Vocal ad lib.)

ca. Up - side,__ in - side out, she's liv - in' la vi - da lo - ca. She'll push and__ pull__ you down, liv - in' la vi - da lo - ca. Her lips are__ dev - il red__ and her skin's the col - or of mo -

cha.   She will wear you out,   liv - in' la vi - da lo -

ca,   liv - in' la vi - da lo - ca.   She's

liv - in' la vi - da lo - ca.

Verse 3:
Woke up in New York City
In a funky, cheap hotel.
She took my heart and she took my money.
She must have slipped me a sleeping pill.

Bridge 2:
She never drinks the water
And makes you order French champagne.
Once you've had a taste of her
You'll never be the same.
Yeah, she'll make you go insane.
(To Chorus:)

QUIT PLAYING GAMES
(With My Heart)

Words and Music by
MAX MARTIN and HERBERT CRICHLOW

Quit Playing Games - 5 - 1

Verse 2:
I live my life the way,
To keep you comin' back to me.
Everything I do is for you,
So what is it that you can't see?
Sometimes I wish I could turn back time,
Impossible as it may seem.
But I wish I could so bad, baby
You better quit playing games with my heart.

MACARENA

Words and Music by
ANTONIO ROMERO and RAFAEL RUIZ

Coro:

Da - le a tu cuer - po a - le - grí - a Ma - ca - re - na que tu cuer - po es pa' dar - le a - le - grí - a y co - sa bue - na.

Macarena - 6 - 1

6.
N.C.

Da - le a tu cuer - po a - le - grí - a Ma - ca - re - na, eh,_____ Ma - ca - re - na.

Verso 3:
Macarena sueña con el Corte inglés
Y se compra los modelos mas modernos.
Le gustaría vivir en Nueva York
Y ligar un novio nuevo.

Puente 2:
Macarena sueña con el Corte inglés
Y se compra los modelos mas modernos.
Le gustaría vivir en Nueva York
Y ligar un novio nuevo.
(Al Coro:)

Verso 4:
Macarena tiene un novio que se llama,
Que se llama de apellido Vitorino.
Y en la jura de bandera del muchacho
Se la dió con dos amigos.

Puente 3:
Macarena tiene un novio que se llama,
Que se llama de apellido Vitorino.
Y en la jura de bandera del muchacho
Se la dió con dos amigos.
(Al Coro:)

MAN! I FEEL LIKE A WOMAN!

Words and Music by
SHANIA TWAIN and R.J. LANGE

Verse 1:

Man! I Feel Like a Woman! - 6 - 1

Verse 3:
The girls need a break.
Tonight we're gonna take
The chance to get out on the town.
We don't need romance.
We only wanna dance.
We're gonna let our hair hang down.
The best thing about being a woman
Is the prerogative to have a little fun and...
(To Chorus:)

From the Miramax Motion Picture "Music Of The Heart"

MUSIC OF MY HEART

Words and Music by
DIANE WARREN

done for my__ soul._____ You'll nev - er know__ the gift__ you've__
see - ing me__ through._____ You were the song__ that al - ways__

__ giv - en me._____ I'll car - ry it with me._____
__ made me sing._____ I'm sing - ing this for you._____

Through the days__ a - head,__ I think__ of days__ be - fore,__ when you made me
Ev - 'ry - where__ I go,____ I think____ of where__ I've been__ and of the

Music of My Heart - 6 - 6

RUN-AROUND

Words and Music by
JOHN POPPER

Run-Around - 8 - 1

201

Run-Around - 8 - 4

me___ down?

Repeat ad lib. and fade

Verse 2:
And shake me and my confidence
About a great many things.
But I've been there, I can see it cower
Like a nervous magician waiting in the wings.
Of a bad play where the heroes are right,
And nobody thinks or expects too much,
And Hollywood's calling for the movie rights,
Singing, "Hey babe, let's keep in touch,
Hey baby, let's keep in touch."

Pre-Chorus:
But I want more than a touch,
I want you to reach me,
And show me all the things no one else can see.
So what you feel becomes mine as well,
And soon if we're lucky we'd be unable to tell
What's yours and mine, the fishing's fine,
And it doesn't have to rhyme, so don't you
Feed me a line.
(To Chorus:)

Verse 3:
Tra-lala bomba, dear this is the pilot speaking
And I've got some news for you.
It seems my ship still stands no matter what you drop,
And there ain't a whole lot that you can do.
Oh sure, the banner may be torn
And the wind's gotten colder and perhaps I've grown a little cynical,
But I know no matter what the waitress brings
I shall drink in and always be full
My cup shall always be full.

Pre-Chorus:
Oh, I like coffee and I like tea,
I'd like to be able to enter a final plea,
I still got this dream that you just can't shake.
I love you to the point you can no longer take.
Well alright, okay, so be that way.
I hope and pray that there's something left to say.
(To Chorus:)

Run-Around - 8 - 8

SAVE THE BEST FOR LAST

Words and Music by
WENDY WALDMAN, JON LIND
and PHIL GALDSTON

Save the Best for Last - 5 - 1

Save the Best for Last - 5 - 2

208

Save the Best for Last - 5 - 3

210

SMOOTH

Lyrics by
ROB THOMAS

Music by
ITAAL SHUR and ROB THOMAS

Smooth - 5 - 1

or else for-get a-bout it. Or else for-get a-bout it.

Or else for-get a-bout it.

Repeat ad lib. and fade

Coda
N.C.

Am   F   E7

Am   F   E7

Verse 2:
Well, I'll tell you one thing,
If you would leave, it be a crying shame.
In every breath and every word
I hear your name calling me out, yeah.
Well, out from the barrio,
You hear my rhythm on your radio.
You feel the tugging of the world,
So soft and slow, turning you 'round and 'round.
(To Pre-Chorus:)

From the Original Motion Picture Soundtrack "REALITY BITES"

STAY (I MISSED YOU)

Words and Music by
LISA LOEB

*Gtr. should capo 1st fret if matching the original recording key of D♭.

Stay (I Missed You) - 6 - 1

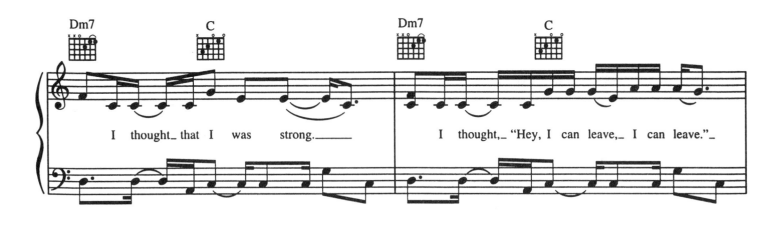

I thought_ that I was strong._____

I thought,_ "Hey, I can leave,_ I can leave."_

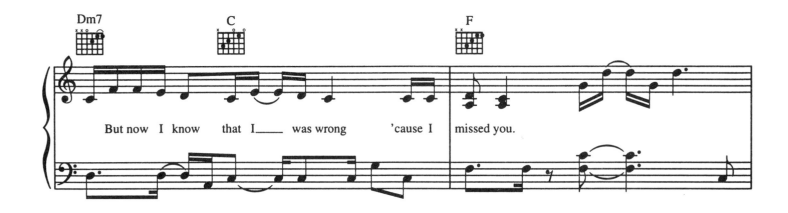

But now I know that I_____ was wrong 'cause I missed you.

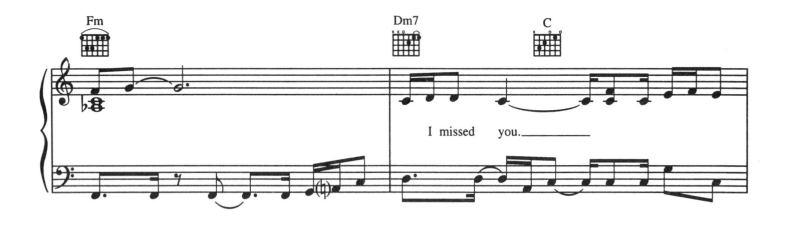

I missed you._____

You said, "You caught me 'cause you want me and one day I'll let you go." You try to

THIS KISS

Words and Music by
ROBIN LERNER, ANNIE ROBOFF
and BETH NIELSEN CHAPMAN

Bridge:

You can kiss me in the moon - light, on the roof - top, un - der the sky,_____ oh.

You can kiss me with the win - dows o - pen while the rain comes blow-in' in - side,_____ oh.

Kiss me in sweet, slow mo - tion. Let's let ev - 'ry-thing slide._____

You got me float - ing, you got me fly - ing.

This Kiss - 4 - 4

2 BECOME 1

Words and Music by
SPICE GIRLS, MATTHEW ROWEBOTTOM
and RICHARD STANNARD

1. Can-dle light_ and soul_ for-ev - er a dream of you and me_ to-ge - ther.
(Verse 2 see block lyric)

Say you be-lieve_ it, say you be-lieve_ it. Free your mind_ of doubt_ and dan - ger,

2 Become 1 - 5 - 1

be a lit-tle bit wis-er ba-by,____ put it on, put it on,____ 'cause to-night____

____ is the night____ when two be-come one.____ I

need some love like I nev-er need-ed love be-fore,___ (wan-na make love to ya ba-by.) I

had a lit-tle love, now I'm back for more, (wan-na make love to ya ba-by.) I

2 Become 1 - 5 - 4

Verse 2:

Silly games that you were playing, empty words we both were saying,
Let's work it out boy, let's work it out boy.
Any deal that we endeavour, boys and girls feel good together,
Take it or leave it, take it or leave it.
Are you as good as I remember baby, get it on, get it on,
'Cause tonight is the night when two become one.

I need some love like I never needed love before, (wanna make love to ya baby.)
I had a little love, now I'm back for more, (wanna make love to ya baby.)
Set your spirit free, it's the only way to be.

UN-BREAK MY HEART

Words and Music by
DIANE WARREN

Un-Break My Heart - 5 - 1

Come back and bring back my smile, come and take these tears a-way. I
Don't leave me here with these tears, come and kiss this pain a-way. I

need your arms to hold me now. Nights are so un-kind.
can't for-get the day you left. Time is so un-kind,

Bring back those nights when I held you be-side me.
and life is so cruel with-out you here be-side me. } Un-break my heart,

%% Chorus:

say you love me a-gain. Un-do this hurt.

Lyrics: you caused when you walked out the door and walked out of my life. Un-cry these tears I cried so man-y nights. Un-break my heart.

To Coda

234

VALENTINE

Composed by
JIM BRICKMAN and JACK KUGELL

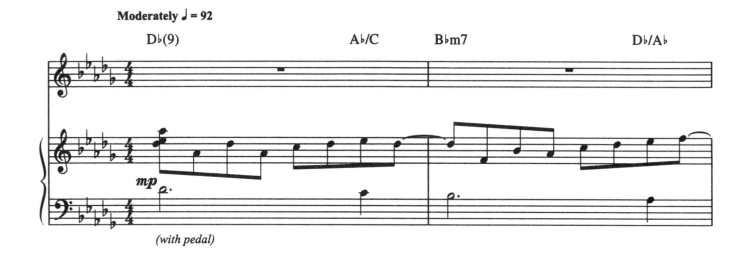

If there were no words,___ no way to speak,___ I

Valentine - 6 - 1

Valentine - 6 - 2

238

Valentine - 6 - 3

240

WAITING FOR TONIGHT

Words and Music by MICHAEL GARVIN,
MARIA CHRISTENSEN and PHIL TEMPLE

Waiting for Tonight - 5 - 1

Verse:

1. Like a mov-ie scene,___ in the sweet-est dreams,___ I have pic-tured us to-
2. Ten-der words you say___ take my breath a - way.___ Love me now and leave me

geth - er.___ Now to feel___ your lips___ on my fin - ger - tips,___
nev - er.___ Found a sa - cred place,___ lost in your___ em - brace.___

I have to say___ is e - ven bet - ter___ than I ev - er thought it___ could
I want to stay___ in this for - ev - er.___ I (2.3.) think of___ the days when___ the

pos - si - bly be. It's per - fect,___ it's pas - sion,___ it's set - ting___ me free from
sun used___ to set on my emp - ty heart, all___ a - lone in___ my bed.

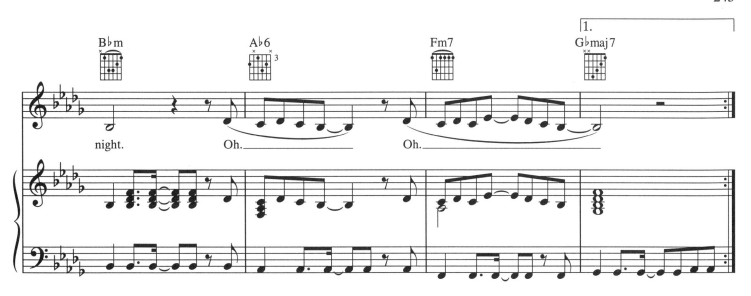

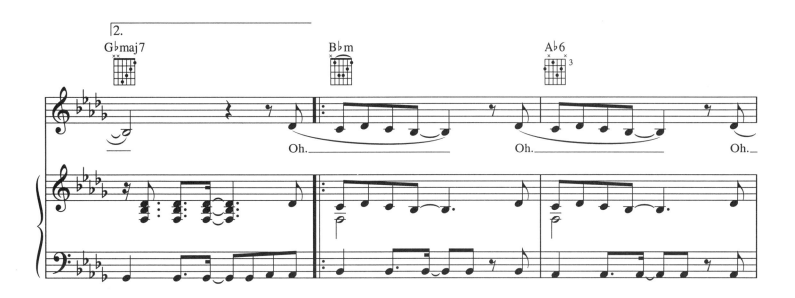

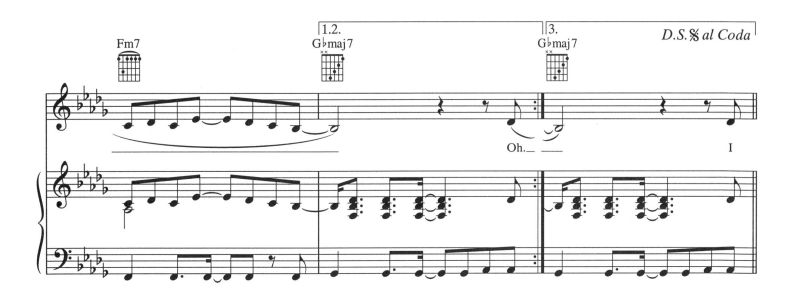

246

WHERE DOES MY HEART BEAT NOW

Words and Music by
TAYLOR RHODES and
ROBERT WHITE JOHNSON

Moderately slow

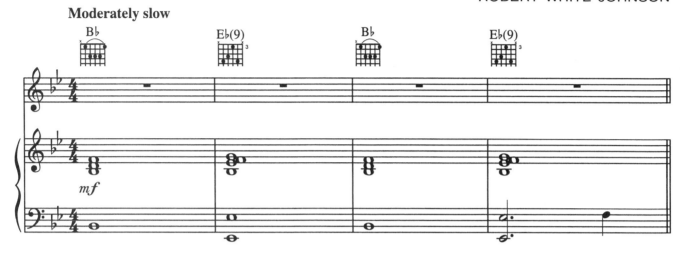

Verse:

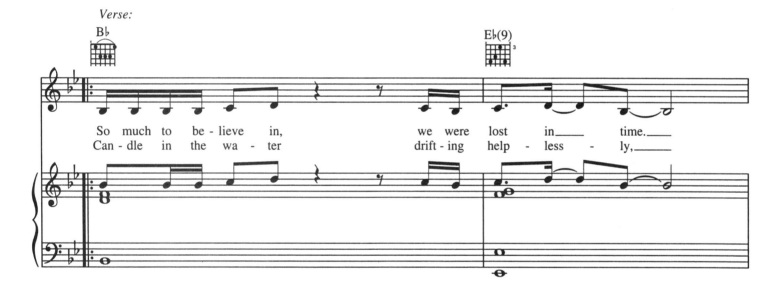

So much to be - lieve in, we were lost in____ time.____
Can - dle in the wa - ter drift - ing help - less - ly,____

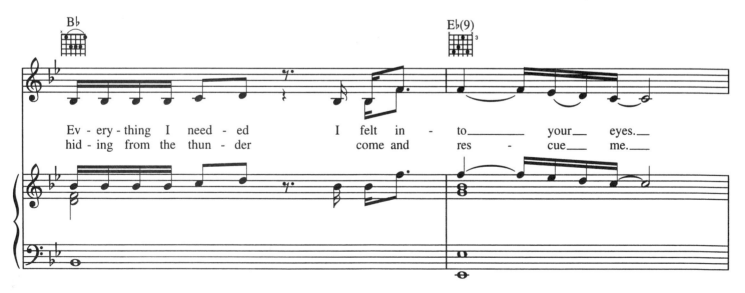

Ev - ery - thing I need - ed I felt in - to____ your____ eyes.____
hid - ing from the thun - der come and res - cue____ me.

Where Does My Heart Beat Now - 5 - 1

FINALLY

Words and Music by
CE CE PENISTON, E.L. LINNEAR,
RODNEY KAY JACKSON and FELIPE DELGADO

254

Finally - 6 - 3

ee, da da ee, ya ya ee, ah woo. Dum da ee, da da ee, ya ya ee, ah woo. Dum da

ee, da da ee, ya ya ee, ah woo. Dum da ee, da da ee, ya ya ee, ah woo.

D.S. %

Verse 2:
It seemed so many times
He seemed to be the one,
But all he ever wanted was to
Have a little fun.
But now you come along
And brighten up my world.
In my heart, I feel it;
I'm that special kind of girl.
Finally, you come along.
The way I feel about ya,
It just can't be wrong.
If you only knew
The way I feel about you.
I just can't describe it, oh, no, no.
(To Chorus:)

100 years of Popular Music

Celebrate All the Classic Hits of the 20th Century with This New Series from Warner Bros. Publications

1900 (MFM0306)

Eighty-nine hits from 1900 to 1920 in one collection! Aba Daba Honeymoon • Alexander's Ragtime Band • The Band Played On • A Bicycle Built for Two • Bill Bailey, Won't You Please Come Home? • Danny Boy • The Entertainer • Give My Regards to Broadway • Meet Me in St. Louis, Louis • Over There • Take Me Out to the Ball Game • When Irish Eyes Are Smiling • When the Saints Go Marching In • You're a Grand Old Flag, and many more.

1920 (MFM0307)

More than 250 pages of classic songs from the Roaring Twenties! Ain't We Got Fun • The Birth of the Blues • Bye Bye Blackbird • The Charleston • Clap Yo' Hands • Fascinating Rhythm • Get Happy • Hard-Hearted Hannah • I'm Just Wild About Harry • Ma! (He's Making Eyes at Me) • Makin' Whoopee! • Ol' Man River • 'S Wonderful • Singin' in the Rain • The Varsity Drag, and many more.

1930 (MFM0308)

A smokin' collection of favorites from the thirties! Ain't Misbehavin' • A-Tisket, A-Tasket • Begin the Beguine • Bei Mir Bist Du Schön • Embraceable You • A Fine Romance • Forty-Second Street • Hooray for Hollywood • I Got Rhythm • I've Got a Crush on You • Jeepers Creepers • Let's Call the Whole Thing Off • Lullaby of Broadway • My Heart Belongs to Daddy • Over the Rainbow • Summertime • The Way You Look Tonight, and many more.

1940 (MFM0309)

From the swingin' forties comes this incredible collection! Beat Me Daddy, Eight to the Bar • Bewitched • Body and Soul • Boogie Woogie Bugle Boy • Chattanooga Choo Choo • How High the Moon • I've Got a Gal in Kalamazoo • New York, New York • On Green Dolphin Street • Pennsylvania 6-5000 • 'Round Midnight • You Make Me Feel So Young, and many more.

1950 (MFM0310)

Catch all the smooth stylings and rock 'n' roll of the fifties! Blue Suede Shoes • Catch a Falling Star • Chances Are • Earth Angel • Enchanted • Good Golly Miss Molly • Great Balls of Fire • Mack the Knife • Only You (And You Alone) • Que Sera, Sera • (We're Gonna) Rock Around the Clock • Smoke Gets in Your Eyes • Splish Splash • Tammy • The Twelfth of Never, and many more.

1960 (MFM0311)

Collect all the soulful tunes of the sixties! Be My Baby • Brown-Eyed Girl • California Dreamin' • Chain of Fools • Crying • The Girl from Ipanema • I Say a Little Prayer • I Want to Hold Your Hand • It's Not Unusual • Let's Twist Again • Na Na Hey Hey Kiss Him Goodbye • Oh, Pretty Woman • Poetry in Motion • Proud Mary, and many more.

1970 (MFM0312)

Rock out with these great tunes from the seventies! All by Myself • American Pie • Can't Get Enough of Your Love, Babe • Dancing Queen • I Will Survive • If You Love Me (Let Me Know) • Killing Me Softly with His Song • Old Time Rock & Roll • Sister Golden Hair • Sweet Home Alabama • You're So Vain, and many more.

1980 (MFM0313)

All the unforgettable hits of the Me Decade! 1-2-3 • Addicted to Love • Arthur's Theme • Beat It • Call Me • Maneater • Morning Train (Nine to Five) • Owner of a Lonely Heart • The Safety Dance • She Works Hard for the Money • That's What Friends Are For • What's Love Got to Do with It • We Built This City • You Give Love a Bad Name, and many more.

1990 (MFM0314)

The hottest hits of the last decade! All for Love • All I Wanna Do • Believe • Dreaming of You • From This Moment On • Have I Told You Lately • Hold On • How Do I Live • I Will Always Love You • Insensitive • Ironic • Livin' la Vida Loca • Macarena • Save the Best for Last • Smooth • Stay (I Missed You) • Un-Break My Heart • Waiting for Tonight • Where Does My Heart Beat Now, and many more.

2000 (MFM0315)

All the modern hits of the new millennium so far! Bye Bye Bye • Can't Get You Out of My Head • Come on Over (All I Want Is You) • Complicated • Cry Me a River • Dilemma • Everywhere • Hero • Hey Baby • I'm Like a Bird • Love Don't Cost a Thing • Music • Show Me the Meaning of Being Lonely • Thank You • A Thousand Miles, and many more.

All editions are arranged for Piano/Vocal/Chords

AD1116 07/03

TEN YEARS OF MUSIC HISTORY
REMEMBERING THE '90s SERIES

This series is an anthology of music from 1990-2000.
Each volume includes artists' works and biographies!

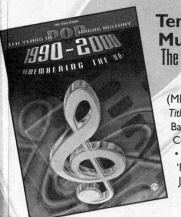

Ten Years of Pop Music History
The Red Book

(MFM0004)

Titles include: All for Love • Always Be My Baby • ...Baby One More Time • Believe • Coming Out of the Dark • Foolish Games • Here I Am (Come and Take Me) • How 'Bout Us • I Don't Want to Miss a Thing • Just Another Day • (God Must Have Spent) A Little More Time on You • More Than Words • Music of My Heart • Show Me the Way • Smooth • Something to Talk About • That's the Way It Is • Un-Break My Heart • You Were Meant for Me and many more.

Ten Years of Pop Music History
The Blue Book

(MFM0005)

Titles include: Back at One • Because You Loved Me • Breakfast at Tiffany's • Change the World • Constant Craving • Don't Cry for Me Argentina • Dreaming of You • From a Distance • Genie in a Bottle • I Do (Cherish You) • I Will Always Love You • If It Makes You Happy • Ironic • Killing Me Softly • Larger Than Life • Love Is All Around • Love Will Keep Us Alive • One of Us • Sunny Came Home and many more.

Ten Years of Country Music History
The Orange Book

(MFM0006)

Titles include: Angels Among Us • Any Man of Mine • A Bad Goodbye • Don't Take the Girl • Forever's As Far As I'll Go • From Here to Eternity • Go Away, No Wait a Minute • I Can Love You Like That • I Cross My Heart • I Do (Cherish You) • I Swear • I'd Like to Have That One Back • If Tomorrow Never Comes • The River • This Kiss • A Thousand Miles from Nowhere • Unanswered Prayers • When You Say Nothing at All • You Light Up My Life and many more.

Ten Years of Country Music History
The Green Book

(MFM0007)

Titles include: Amazed • Breathe • Commitment • The Dance • From This Moment On • How Do I Live • In Another's Eyes • My Maria • Please Remember Me • Pocket of a Clown • Put Yourself in My Shoes • Something in Red • Standing Outside the Fire • Strawberry Wine • There's Your Trouble • 26¢ • Two Sparrows in a Hurricane • What Might Have Been • Years From Here and many more.

Ten Years of Movie Music History
The Yellow Book

(MFM0009)

Titles include: Against the Wind (from *Forest Gump*) • At the Beginning (from *Anastasia*) • Don't Cry for Me Argentina (from *Evita*) • I Believe I Can Fly (from *Space Jam*) • I Say a Little Prayer (from *My Best Friend's Wedding*) • Music of My Heart (from *Music of the Heart*) • The Prayer (from *Quest for Camelot*) • Take Me to the River (from *The Commitments*) • Theme from *Jurassic Park* • There's Something About Mary (from *There's Something About Mary*) and many more.

Ten Years of Movie Music History
The Purple Book

(MFM0010)

Titles include: Anyone at All (from *You've Got Mail*) • Colors of the Wind (from *Pocahontas*) • Duel of the Fates (from *Star Wars: Episode 1 The Phantom Menace*) • I Will Remember You (from *The Brothers McMullen*) • Kissing You (Love Theme from *Romeo + Juliet*) • Once in a Lifetime (from *Only You*) • Something to Talk About (from *Something to Talk About*) • That Thing You Do (from *That Thing You Do!*) • Uninvited (from *City of Angels*) and many more.

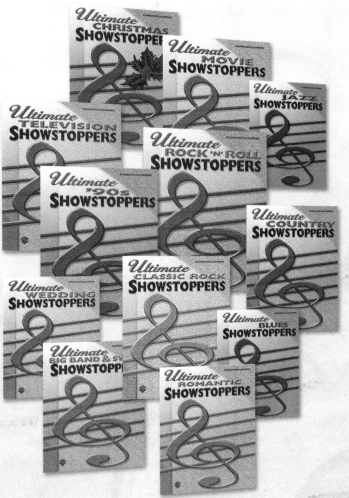